Fix It!

Matching and Sorting

by Lynn Maslen Kertell
pictures by Sue Hendra and John R. Maslen

Scholastic Inc.
New York • Toronto • London • Auckland • Sydney • Mexico City • New Delhi • Hong Kong • Buenos Aires

Sally and Seth were
going on a play date.

They went to Tanner's house.

Sally found a broken drum.
She asked Tanner's brother,
"Sam, can you fix it?"

What do they need to fix the drum?

Sam and Sally fixed the drum.

Seth's flag was broken.
"Can you fix it, Sam?" he asked.

"Sure," said Sam,
"what does it need?"

It needed a new stick.
"That should do it," said Seth.

Tanner's tricycle didn't work.
"What do we need to fix it?"
wondered Tanner.

"A new wheel!" yelled Tanner.
"That's just what it needed!"

Hooray! The toys were fixed
and everyone could play!